Outdoor Crafts

Lots of fun things to make and do outside

A Dorling Kindersley Book

DK

LONDON, NEW YORK,
MELBOURNE, MUNICH, and DELHI

Senior designer Sonia Whillock-Moore
Senior editors Deborah Lock, Penny Smith, and Carrie Love
Designers Jessica Bentall, Gemma Fletcher, Rachael Grady, Hedi Hunter, Rosie Levine, Sadie Thomas, Pamela Shiels, Mary Sandberg, Gabriela Rosecka, Lauren Rosier
Additional editing Wendy Horobin, Lee Wilson, Lorrie Mack, Holly Beaumont
US editor Margaret Parrish
Photographer Will Heap
Additional photography Craig Robertson
Food stylists Denise Smart and Annie Nichols
Picture researchers Rob Nunn
Consultant Simon Maughan
Food consultant Jill Bloomfield
Category publisher Mary Ling
Production editor Sean Daly, Clare McLean, and Tony Phipps
Production controllers Seyhan Esen and Claire Pearson
Jacket designer Rosie Levine

First published in the United States in 2013
by DK Publishing, 375 Hudson Street, New York, New York 10014

Material used in this book was previously published in:
Grow It, Cook It (2008), *Ready, Steady, Grow!* (2010), and
How Does My Garden Grow? (2011)

Copyright © 2013 Dorling Kindersley Limited
13 14 15 16 17 10 9 8 7 6 5 4 3 2 1
191999—05/2013

DK books are available at special discounts when purchased in bulk for sales promotions, premiums, fund-raising, or educational use. For details contact: DK Publishing Special Markets, 375 Hudson Street, New York, New York 10014 SpecialSales@DK.com

A catalog record for this book is available from the Library of Congress.
ISBN 978-1-4654-0824-2
Printed and bound by South China in China

Discover more at
www.dk.com

Contents

Sun symbol guide
What the lighting terms mean:

Full sun   Partial sun   Shade

For full sun, the plant needs 6 hours of direct sunlight each day. For partial sun, the plant needs 4-6 hours of direct sunlight each day. For shade, the plant needs very little direct sunlight, or none at all.

Soil-type symbols

Dry soil

Moist soil

Wet soil

Germination symbols

1 week

1-2 weeks

2-3 weeks

3-4 weeks

Introduction

This book is full of ideas of things you can do. The MAKE IT section shows you how to create labels and markers to use in your garden. It also demonstrates how to make a scarecrow-like garden buddy, painted pots, dazzling decorations, and creative containers.

Learn how to turn plants into food in the COOK IT section. Herbs become muffins, pumpkins are the main ingredient in pies, potatoes and carrots are turned into chips, lemons are changed into ice pops, and blueberries are used in the most delicious cheesecake.

Transform plants into fantastic projects in the CREATE IT section. Set up an enchanted path, a window box wildlife container, a Wild-West cacti land, an ivy man, corn paper, and a container pond.

Make It

What is a plant?

A plant is a living thing that feeds, grows, and produces new plants. There are nearly 400,000 different types of plant. They all have the same basic parts—leaves, stems, flowers, and roots.

Terminal bud
The main growing point of the plant.

Bees
and other insects help pollinate flowers.

Leaves

The leaves are where the plant captures energy from sunlight and uses it to turn nutrients into food. They are covered in tiny openings that let gases and moisture in and out of the plant.

Flowers

Many plants reproduce using flowers. Once the flowers have been fertilized, they produce seeds or fruit. Most nonflowering plants use their leaves, stems, or roots to make new plants.

Fruit

Stem

Stems support the leaves and flowers. They act as a transportation network to take water, minerals, and food to all parts of the plant. They have growing points along their length that produce leaves and new shoots.

Roots

Roots anchor the plant to its surroundings. They also suck up water and nutrients that the plant needs to grow. Sometimes roots are used to store food and water.

Root hairs
These take up most of the water from the soil.

Root tip
This is the part of the root that grows.

How do plants grow?

Seed leaf

True leaf

Here we go!

Most flowering plants begin life as a seed. Seeds are little packages that contain everything a new plant needs to grow—the baby plant itself and food to get it started.

Seeds will only start to grow when the conditions are right. The seed takes in water, which makes it swell and split the seed case. The main root emerges and reaches down into the soil.

The seed then sends up one or two tiny leaves. These are called cotyledons, or seed leaves. These are quickly followed by the first true leaves. The seedling can now begin to make its own food.

Flowers: the inside story

Seeds form inside flowers. If you slice down through a flower you will see that at the base is a swollen chamber called the ovary. Leading to the ovary is a tube called the style, which has a sticky end called a stigma. Pollen is carried onto the stigma by the wind or insects. The pollen travels down the style to fertilize the ovules. The flower then falls off and the fruit starts to grow.

Flowers also use scent to attract pollinators.

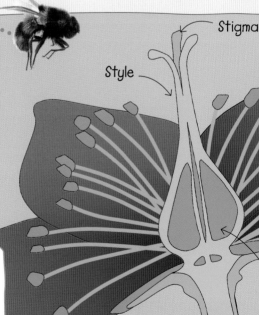

Stigma

Style

Stamens
These produce pollen grains.

Ovary
This contains the ovules, which become the seeds.

Petals
are colored to attract insects.

Labels and markers

Whenever you plant seeds, remember to make a label. When seedlings appear, it can get very confusing to identify which plant is which. Your labels can be as simple as ice-pop sticks with names written on them, or you can have some fun making and decorating your own.

Some vegetables and fruits have many varieties and each one will be different. Look for the variety on the seed packet and include it on your label.

Stone markers

Mark the pots that you have used with colorful stones. What eye-catching designs will you paint?

Why not paint a stone in one color and then choose another color for a flower, or paint the first letter of your name?

Paint

Tall labels

Labels on sticks will stand out in a pot. They are ideal markers for plants that will grow tall and bushy, such as herbs. Waterproof labels can be made using pizza bases, which are also easy to cut and paint.

You will need:

Recycle a pizza base

Skewers

Reuse an old plastic bottle

1. Carefully cut off the bottom of your bottle.

2. Cut a small circle out of your pizza base.

3. Push the skewer inside the circle and glue to the bottle base.

4. Now decorate your flower.

Basil

Butterfly

1. Draw a butterfly on a pizza base. Cut it out.

2. Push your stick inside the butterfly. Now it's ready to paint.

Ice-pop labels

Ice-pop sticks are very handy as labels for small seed pots. Use pens to draw a picture of the vegetable you have planted or to make a striped pattern in the same color as the vegetable.

You can also use a clothes pin to label your seedling.

Paint the end of a stick to measure how deep to make your seed hole.

⅓ in (1cm)

¾ in (2cm)

1⅛ in (3cm)

Leek

11

More plant labels

Use old **buttons** to decorate your labels.

Here are more ways you can help yourself remember what you plant. These jazzy plant labels will brighten up your garden. You can also make up your own designs using recycled odds and ends from home.

Flower power

Use an old **CD**, **plastic milk carton**, **pipe cleaner**, and **buttons** to make this dazzling label. Its shiny surface will also scare birds away. Glue everything together with a quick-setting, waterproof glue.

1. **Start by** cutting petal shapes out of the plastic carton. Glue them to the back of the CD, overlapping them slightly.

2. **Turn the CD over** and decorate with buttons and a pipe cleaner. Finish by attaching the flower to a bamboo stick.

Recycled **plastic spoons and forks** make perfect bodies and spiked legs for these garden helpers.

Red lettuce

Pipe cleaners make good legs and antennae.

Sprinkle on **glitter** to add bling to your creations.

Plastic spoons and forks make great bodies.

Cut up **plastic cartons** to make wings and things. The plastic is soft and strong.

Plastic straws make bendable body parts, such as knees and elbows.

bubble wrap wings

plastic yogurt container

Garden helpers

Use washed pieces of packaging, such as **plastic cups**, and **foil food trays** to personalize your helpers.

Lettuce

Sage

Creative containers

Make it ✂

Unusual containers for your plants will make your gardening projects interesting. Any object that has sides can be used, so keep a look out for possible ones to recycle and reuse.

Top tip

When deciding what container would be best to use, think about the height and space the plants will need when they are fully grown.

Recycle food and drink containers.

Old boots or shoes

Use objects in a different way.

Wheelbarrow

Reuse old and broken objects.

Old buckets

Why not use old juice cartons?

14

Get ahead

If you can start early in the spring when the weather is still cold, get the seeds germinating indoors in these newspaper seed pots.

1 **Take a page** from a newspaper or comic. Fold over one long edge, twice. Roll the paper around a glass.

2 **Fold** the overlapping end of the tube inside the glass. This will become the base. Slide the paper off the glass.

3 **Looking** inside the tube, fold down the overlapping ends to make a base. Use the glass to flatten the base against a table.

4 **Fill the pot with soil** and then it is ready for sowing the seeds.

The newspaper pots will disintegrate when planted in the ground.

5 **Once the weather** is warmer outside, the seedlings can be planted in their newspaper pots straight into the soil, without disturbing their roots.

Get prepared

Whatever container you use, prepare it by following these steps:

1 **Ask an adult** to make some holes in the bottom to allow excess water to seep out. Use a liner with holes in if needed.

You can also use the pieces of expanded polystyrene that come with small plants bought from garden centers.

2 **Put a layer** of gravel or broken pots in the base. This stops the soil from running out of the holes with the water.

3 **Fill the container** with suitable potting soil. Most plants are happy with multipurpose potting soil, but some have specific requirements.

15

Seed-box organize

Many of the plants you grow in your garden produce seeds, which you can collect and plant the following year. The secret of success is to collect the seeds at the right time and store them in the right way.

Sunflower seeds

can be collected when the seed heads look big, fat, and brown. Cut off the whole seed head, put into a paper bag, and shake or pinch out the seeds.

Best bargain beans

1 Choose a healthy plant in your garden. Wait until the seed heads or seedpods have ripened and are about to split. On a dry, windless day, cut off the entire seed head or pod.

Store seeds in a paper bag

2 Remove the seeds using your fingers. In a warm place, leave the seeds to dry on a piece of paper towel. Label and store the seeds in a cool, dry place until spring.

3 Prepare a pot for sowing your seeds. Some seeds that are very dried out may need to be soaked first to encourage them to swell and germinate.

4 Last year's seeds have become this year's new plant. Why not trade seeds with other gardeners and give some to your friends to plant, too?

Onion seed heads　　Lettuce run to seed　　Fresh bean seeds　　Corn flowers　　Seeds scattering

Make a seed-box organizer

Your seeds need to be looked after when they are stored. What better way to keep them cool, dry, and safe than in your own seed box? If you organize them carefully, you'll know at a glance when to sow them next year.

SUMMER

Sun

SPRING

Green beans

Zucchini　seeds

1 **Find a box** and a lid and wrap both in colorful paper. Cut out some season dividers from cardboard.

2 **Paint a colorful design** on the dividers. When dry, write SPRING SUMMER, and FALL on them to show when to sow the seeds next year.

3 **Decorate small envelopes** using colorful paints. Also, you can draw or glue on your own plant pictures on the front. Once the envelope is dry, put the seeds inside.

Dwarf french beans

Collected on 14th August 2012

Sow in spring

4 **Seal the envelopes** and label them with the names of the fruit or vegetable, its variety, and the date. Place in the organizer and cover with the lid.

17

Garden buddy

Plunder your recycling bin to create a wacky figure that will keep you company, and help keep birds away from your plants. Form his body from tin cans and lids, then add details using plastic, cardboard, and foil. When he's finished, hang him from a tree or tie him to a stake in the ground. First, lay out all your junk and plan where each piece will go.

You will need:

Collection of junk

Garden wire

Wire from a coat hanger

Glue

Scissors

1 **Gather all your cans.** Ask an adult to make a hole in the bottom of each one by twisting in the point of one scissor blade until it punches through.

2 **For the arms and legs,** make a loop in one end of a length of garden wire and twist to secure. Thread the wire through one can and leave the other end loose to connect to the body.

Continue to attach the other pieces in this way.

3 **To attach the next can,** loop a new piece of wire through the first loop before twisting to secure. Then thread this through the next can and make a loop at the other end.

Do the same to attach the arms higher up the body.

4 **For the body,** make holes in opposite sides of a plastic bottle near the bottom. Insert a length of coat hanger wire through them, looping to secure at each end. The legs will hang from this.

5 **For the figure's head,** use a plastic flowerpot, then glue on bottle caps for the eyes and nose. A strip of foil will make nice shiny teeth.

18

Top tip

CDs make shimmering reflections that will discourage hungry birds, so tuck a few of them inside your figure's body.

String for hair

Foil for hands

19

Painting pots

Decorate plastic or terra-cotta pots for your garden using acrylic paint, colored markers, and glittery glue. Make sure you give your pots time to dry before you fill them with potting soil and plants.

You will need:
- metallic markers
- acrylic paint
- paintbrush
- craft glue
- glitter
- paper shapes
- clear craft varnish

Layer-painting a pot

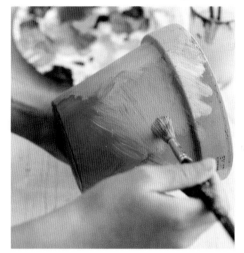

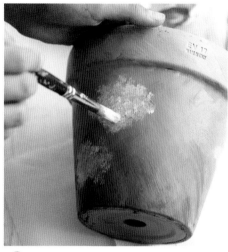

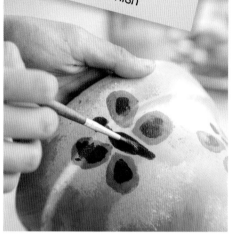

1 **This method** is for a multilayered picture. Brush a dark color on the bottom of the pot and lighter shades toward the top.

2 **Wait for the first coat** to dry, then add another color. We've dabbed on thick paint, straight from the tube, to make clouds.

3 **Add another layer** of paint when the second is dry. We have put butterflies on our pot, but you can add flowers, bugs, or whatever else you like!

Quick polka-dot pot

1 **Stick paper shapes** on your pot. We've used circles, but you can try stars or squares.

2 **Now paint over** the pot and paper circles with acrylic paint. Let it dry.

3 **Peel off** the circles to reveal your pattern. Either leave it plain, or paint the circles in different colors.

Use a silver metallic marker to make a magical night scene on a dark plastic pot.

Add a touch of luxury to a night-time stroll scene using a **golden metallic marker.**

Try mixing **metallic markers** and **acrylic paint** to make a fiery pot for hot crops.

Paint bands of glue on your pot. Sprinkle them with **glitter.** Then repeat with another glittery color.

Use the layer-painting techniques and make up your own designs.

for mom

Don't forget to varnish your paint and glitter pots to make them **weatherproof** and **long-lasting.**

4 **Turn your pot** into a present by adding a name.

Hello

4 **The finished pot**—it hits the spot!

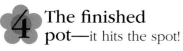

21

Dazzling decorations

Colorful decorations poking up between your plants will not only add sparkle, but can also help to identify what you have planted, like a label. Butterflies, flowers, and bird make pretty decorations. Alternatively, create your own design to suit your garden.

Flower

Bird

Butterfly

Did you know? Plants have two names: a scientific one—often in Latin—and a common name, which may vary from place to place.

You will need:

- clean foil containers
- scissors
- black marker
- colored markers
- skewers
- glue
- pen

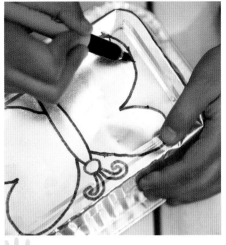

1 **Draw your design** onto the base of a foil container, using a black marker.

2 **Here are some ideas** for your design. You could choose bugs, flowers, and birds.

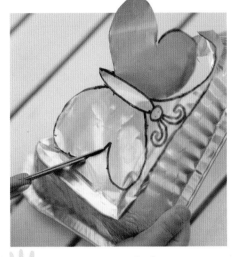

3 **Cut around the outline** of your design using a sharp pair of scissors.

4 **Press a pen** onto the foil shape to make raised holes.

5 **Color your design** with colored permanent markers and let the ink dry.

6 **Spread some glue** down the center of your design where the stick will go.

7 **Attach the stick** and hold it on the glue until it is secure.

8 **Find a place** in your garden to put your colorful butterfly. It would look nice in a window box or flower pot.

Cook It

Herb and cheese muffins

You will need:

- 2¼ cups all-purpose flour
- 1 tbsp baking powder
- 1 tsp salt
- 1 tsp mustard powder
- 5oz (125g) mature Cheddar cheese, grated
- 2 tbsp chopped fresh parsley
- 1 tbsp chopped fresh oregano
- 2 tsp chopped fresh thyme
- freshly ground black pepper
- 2 large eggs
- ¾ cup low-fat milk
- 3oz (75g) butter, melted

yummy

Here is a herb muffin recipe that uses parsley, oregano, and thyme from your garden. The muffins are irresistible and best eaten the day they're made, although they will last for a couple of days.

1 **Preheat the oven** to 375°F (190°C). Line a muffin pan with 10 paper baking cups. Then sift the flour, baking powder, and salt into a bowl.

2 **Add the mustard,** three-quarters of the cheese, and the parsley, oregano, and thyme. Season with black pepper and mix all ingredients together.

3 **In another bowl,** whisk together the eggs, milk, and melted butter, and pour over the dry ingredients.

4 **Stir the mixture** until everything is just combined. Your batter should still be lumpy.

5 **Spoon the batter** into the baking cups, then sprinkle the rest of the cheese on top. Bake for 20–25 minutes, until risen and firm.

Cook it

Basil and tomato muffins
To make these, simply follow the main recipe, but swap the herbs for 2 tbsp chopped fresh basil, and stir in 3oz (75g) chopped sun-dried tomatoes.

Mini pumpkin pies

You'll need

Ask an adult to cut the pumpkin in half with a sharp knife, using a rocking motion. Scoop out the seeds. Slice the pumpkin into pieces, and cut off the peel.

peeled, seeded

1lb 2oz (500g) pumpkin, cut into large chunks

1 tbsp olive oil

cut into 16 pieces

15oz (375g) puff pastry

1 tbsp all-purpose flour

¼ cup molasses

1 whole egg

3 large egg yolks

1½ cups (300 ml) milk

½ split vanilla bean

pinch of salt

Preheat
375°F, 190°C

Roasting time 30–35 mins

Refrigerate for 30 mins

Handy tip!
Baking time 15 mins

1 On a baking sheet, pour olive oil over the pumpkin pieces. Coat them evenly, using your hands. Roast until tender. Cool and then mash with a fork.

2 Shape the puff pastry pieces into balls. Roll out each ball until about 2½in (6cm) in diameter. Press each piece into a muffin pan and put in the fridge.

3 Place a piece of parchment paper into each pastry and fill to the top with baking beans. Bake in the oven then remove the paper and beans.

4 Pour the milk into a pan. Scrape out the vanilla seeds from the bean and add to the milk. Heat the mixture until just below boiling point. Let cool a little.

5 Lightly beat the egg yolks, whole egg, and molasses in a bowl. Add the flour and salt and beat until smooth. Strain the hot milk over the mixture and beat.

6 Pour the smooth mixture into a pan and bring to a boil, stirring constantly until thickened. Remove from heat and stir in the pumpkin puree.

7 Spoon out

the mixture evenly into the pastry crusts. Bake in the oven for 20-25 minutes, until just firm and slightly puffed up. Serve the pies warm, with a dusting of confectioners' sugar on the top if you like.

Lemonade ice pops

Keep cool on a hot summer day with the zingy taste of your juicy lemons. Lemons add flavor to fish and salads as well.

Add slices of lemon to drinks and salads.

You'll need

6 juicy lemons

1 cup honey

3 cups cold water

18 sticks

18 empty yogurt cups

1 **Finely grate** the zest from three of the lemons and place in a pan with the honey and 2 cups water. Bring to a boil, then remove from the heat.

2 **Squeeze the juice** from all of the lemons. Pour into a liquid measuring cup. This should give you about 1 cup of juice.

3 **Strain the honey** and lemon water through a strainer into a bowl. Pour in some lemon juice. Stir and taste. Add more juice until you achieve the taste you want.

Freezing time 1-2 hours

4 **Leave the lemonade** to cool in the fridge. Add the rest of the water to dilute. Stir, then pour into 18 empty yogurt cups. Place in the freezer until partly set.

5 **Push a ice pop stick** into each cup. Return the cups to the freezer until the lemonade becomes completely solid.

6 **Crunch!** Enjoy the cold juicy taste, but be quick—it won't take long for your ice pop to melt on a hot day.

Throw in some ice cubes. Sooo cool!

For a refreshing drink, pour a little of your lemonade (from Step 3) into a glass and top off with cold seltzer.

Herbal sun tea

Important stuff

All these herbs like to grow in full sunlight and use moist, well-drained soil mixed with some grit.

Herbs have been grown all over the world for centuries for their flavor and goodness. Some herbs are used to make healthy refreshing drinks, such as herbal teas. Using the warmth of the Sun during the day, you, too, can make a delicious tea from herbs you've grown or bought.

Which herbs?

Be careful to choose the right parts of each herb to make different sun teas. We used:

Jar 1: The flowers and leaves of bergamot, or bee balm.

Jar 2: The stems and leaves of epazote.

Jar 3: The leaves of mint and lemon verbena together.

Jar 4: The leaves of lemon balm and catnip together.

Jar 5: The leaves of borage.

Jar 6: The leaves of lemongrass cut into 2in (5cm) lengths.

Lemon verbena   Mint

Epazote   Bergamot

1 **Ask an adult** to drill holes in the bottom of an old suitcase. Place a plastic liner inside and punch holes in it. Add a layer of grit and fill the suitcase with potting soil mixed with grit.

2 **Imagine** the surface of your suitcase is a world map. Arrange the herb plants you have bought according to the position of the country where they originated.

Hold the plant by the root ball as you gently remove it from its pot.

3 **For each plant,** make a deep hole in the potting soil that is large enough for the root ball. Water the plant, then gently squeeze it out of its pot and place the plant it into the hole.

4 **Fill in the soil** around the plant. The base of the stem should be level with the soil surface. Once you've planted all your herbs, water them around their roots.

Make flags to show where the herbs originated. For example, borage is native to Syria and epazote to Mexico.

Make sun tea

Shake the jar every now and then throughout the day.

1 **In the morning,** pick 3 to 4 tablespoons of the fresh leaves, flowers, or stems depending on the herb you want to use, and put them into a jar.

2 **Add 2 cups** (½ liter) of water. Put the lid of the jar on securely and shake the mixture well. Leave the jar in a place that gets full sunlight.

3 **In the late afternoon,** the tea should appear a rich green in color and be warm to drink. Strain the contents and serve. Discard any unused tea.

Red currant refreshments

Like glittering rubies, red currants ripen on the bush in spring. Add these juicy jewels to fruit salads or use them in a refreshing drink, like this cordial. If you don't have a red currant bush, buy these gems at a farmers' market or gather them from a pick-your-own farm.

To pick, remove the entire cluster by hand or use scissors to cut off the sprigs.

You will need:

8oz (225g) red currants, stems removed
4oz (100g) raspberries
1¼ cups sugar
2 cups cold water

1 **Ask an adult** to make a syrup by heating the sugar and water slowly in a saucepan, stirring gently until the sugar has dissolved. Boil for 3 minutes, then let cool.

2 **Put the fruit** into a bowl and mash it together well using the back of a fork or a potato masher. Place a damp dish towel under the bowl so it doesn't slip.

4 **Cut the end** off a clean pair of panty hose (make sure they're an old pair) or cut a square of clean cheesecloth and stretch it over a tall pitcher. Secure with a rubber band.

5 **Pour the fruit mixture** through the hose or cloth, which will act like a fine sieve and allow only the juice to pass through and collect in the bowl underneath. let this stand for an hour or two.

6 **Mix the rest** of the cooled syrup with the cordial. Pour the mixture into a clean bottle and store it in the fridge until you need it.

A bush of your own . . .

Buy a young bush and plant it in a large container or directly into the ground. Choose a sunny open spot with a little shade. After a year or two, if you look after your plant, red currants will grow in abundance year after year.

In **early spring**, add a mulch of well-rotted compost to keep in the moisture and prevent weeds. Feed with a high-potash fertilizer.
In **spring**, before the fruit ripens, cover the bush with a net to keep hungry birds away.

In **fall**, once the plant is established, take cuttings to grow more bushes. Choose strong, straight stems with lots of buds, and trim into 4–6in (10–15cm) lengths. Push into soil in a small pot, leaving a little above the surface. Keep them moist, and in the spring they will start to grow.

Plant your cuttings into their own pots in the following fall. After four years, every **winter**, prune out two or three of the oldest branches.

3 **Into your mashed** fruit, pour ½ cup of the sugary syrup that was prepared earlier. Stir this mixture gently, but thoroughly.

7 **When you're ready,** pour a little cordial into a pitcher according to taste and add water, sparkling water, or soda water to make a refreshing treat.

Pepper hummus

Here's a recipe for red pepper hummus. And if you have any spare bell peppers, use them to make delicious little serving dishes.

You will need:

- 2 red bell peppers
- ¾ cup canned chickpeas
- 1 tsp paprika
- 1 clove garlic, peeled
- juice of ½ lemon
- 1 tbsp tahini
- 3 tbsp olive oil
- salt and pepper
- bell pepper shells, to serve

1 Cut each pepper into 4 and remove the stems and seeds. Preheat the broiler.

2 Line a broiler pan with foil and place the bell peppers skin-side up. Broil for 5 minutes, or until the skins have blackened.

3 Put the hot peppers into a plastic bag and seal it. When the peppers are cool enough to handle, peel off the blackened skins.

4 Put the bell peppers, chickpeas, paprika, garlic, lemon juice, tahini, and olive oil in a food processor and blend until smooth. Season to taste.

5 Spoon the hummus into the bell pepper shells and serve.

Remove my seeds before you use me as a pot.

Top tip

Serve the hummus with pita bread and carrot and cucumber sticks. Don't forget to eat the bell pepper containers!

Potato and carrot chips

Use homegrown potatoes and carrots to make delicious oven-baked chips. Once you've made these, experiment with other vegetables, like parsnips and beets.

You will need:

For the potato chips

- 2 medium potatoes
- 2 tsp sunflower oil
- salt and pepper
- 1–2 tsp paprika (optional)

For the carrot chips

- 2 medium carrots
- 2 tsp sunflower oil
- 2 tsp honey
- salt and pepper

1 **For the potato chips,** preheat the oven to 350°F (180°C). Slice the potatoes using a peeler. Mix them with the oil, salt, pepper, and paprika, if using.

2 **Line a baking sheet** with parchment paper. Arrange the potato slices in a single layer. Cook for 10 minutes, turn them over, and cook for another 10 minutes.

2 **Line a baking sheet** with parchment paper. Arrange the carrots in a single layer and cook for 10 minutes. Turn the chips over and cook for another 7–10 minutes.

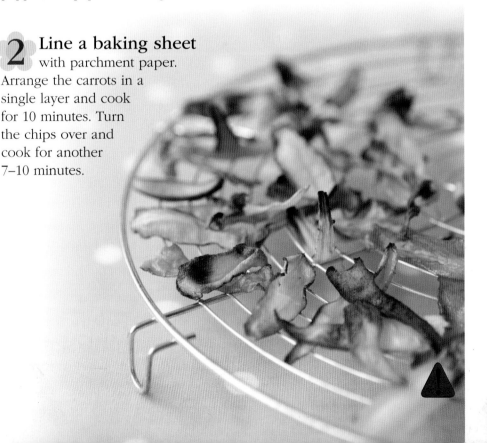

1 **For the carrot chips,** preheat the oven to 350°F (180°C). Use a vegetable peeler to slice the carrots thinly. Mix them with the oil, honey, salt, and pepper.

Top tip

Keep your eye on the chips as they cook and remove them from the oven when they turn golden. Cool on a wire rack.

Blueberry cheesecake

You can grow blueberries in your garden. They taste delicious in cheesecake. Try eating them with yogurt, or add them to muffin mixes or smoothies.

You'll need

1lb (500g) blueberries

2 tbsp super-fine sugar

1 cup cream cheese

1 cup crème fraîche

¼ tsp pure vanilla extract

8 oat cookies, crushed

More blueberry recipes

Try adding them to pancakes

Make yummy blueberry smoothies

They also taste great in muffins!

1 **Place ¾ of the berries** and ½ the sugar into a small saucepan. Cover and simmer for five minutes, until soft. Stir in the other berries and let cool.

2 **Using a wooden spoon**, beat the cream cheese, crème fraîche, remaining sugar, and vanilla extract together in a mixing bowl. Continue until well mixed and soft.

3 **Fill four glasses** with a spoonful of the blueberry sauce, then a spoonful of the cream-cheese mixture, followed by a spoonful of crushed cookies.

4 **Repeat the layers** once more and then put the filled glasses in the fridge for an hour.

The blueberry is one of the few fruits native to North America. Some Native Americans call it a star berry because the white flowers are shaped like five-pointed stars.

Colorful kebabs

Jewel-bright skewers of garden vegetables make an ideal summer snack. Zucchini are a winner for being one of the easiest members of the squash family to grow. You can also grow bell peppers in your garden to use in kebabs and other dishes.

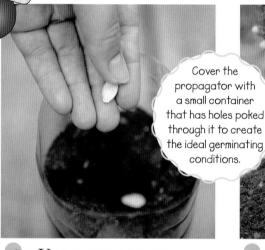

Cover the propagator with a small container that has holes poked through it to create the ideal germinating conditions.

1 Use a propagator to grow your seeds. Make a ½in (1.5cm) deep hole, then push two seeds (on their sides) into the hole. When the seedlings appear, pull out the weakest one.

2 Once the seedling has grown, dig out a hole in a large prepared container. Squeeze the bottle to remove the plant. Place the plant in the hole, firm the soil around it, and water well.

3 Add mulch around the plant to help the soil stay moist and weed free. Make sure the mulch doesn't touch the stem.

A fungus called powdery mildew can appear on zucchini plant leaves. Avoid this by keeping your plants well-watered, fed, and with space around them for good airflow.

4 A zucchini plant needs constantly moist soil, so bury a 6in (15cm) pot that has holes in the bottom next to the plant. Frequently water into the pot so that water will flow directly to the roots.

5 When the first flowers begin to form, feed the plant every 10–14 days with a tomato fertilizer and some compost tea. Do not overfeed.

6 When the zucchini are 4in (10cm) long, cut them at their base. This will encourage more zucchini to grow on your plant.

Top tip

Another good recipe is to grate zucchini and mix the gratings with a whisked egg, onion, and grated cheese mixture. Fry the mixture in a frying pan until light brown on both sides.

Create a kebab

Planning a barbecue, or need a tasty side dish? Then try out this colorful kebab.

1 **Carefully** thread some slices of yellow bell pepper, zucchini, and baby corn and some cherry tomatoes onto some skewers or kebab sticks.

2 **Using** a pastry brush, baste the vegetables with some olive oil before placing them onto a grill pan or barbecue, or under the broiler. Watch them and ask an adult to turn them over a few times during cooking so that the vegetables brown all over.

Create It

Fairy ring

Grow a secret fairy ring in a hidden spot in the backyard. You never know, you might attract some fairies! A circle of ornamental grasses, along with delicate sweet-smelling flowers, looks magical and makes a great place to play or have a picnic. Don't forget the fairy cakes!

You will need:

Ornamental grasses and a selection of unusually shaped flowers

Jars and glass paints or household paint and varnish

Tea lights

> Walk around, dragging the stick firmly into the ground to mark the edge of the circle.

1 **Make a circular** area by sticking a stake where you'd like the middle of the ring to be. Tie a long piece of string to this and tie another stake to the other end and use this to mark the edge.

2 **Use a shovel** to dig out a deep trench around the edge of the circle and sprinkle potting soil into the base. Put the turf that you have taken out onto a compost heap.

> Reuse the soil that was removed when digging the trench or use fresh potting soil.

3 **Gently remove** each plant from its pot and place it into the trench. Fill soil around the plant's roots, pressing the soil down firmly to keep it upright.

4 **Water all the plants** well and add a decorative mulch if you wish. Continue to water the plants well during the first few weeks.

5 **Make pretty lanterns** by painting jars using special glass paint (or household paint and a layer of varnish). Place tea lights inside the jars and ask an adult to light them in the evening.

You can also add sparkly solar night-lights to light the fairy ring. They come on automatically at dusk.

When it rains, cover the jars with plastic.

47

Flowerpot people

Bright, sunny sunflowers look pretty in a pot. You can make them look even more cheerful by painting the pot and giving them a smiley face. For quick results, use dwarf sunflower seeds, but if you want to grow a pot person that's taller than you, use other varieties and a bigger pot.

Important stuff

Grow sunflowers in a place that gets full sun. Use well-drained soil. Seeds will germinate in 2–3 weeks and flowers will open after 7–10 weeks.

You will need:

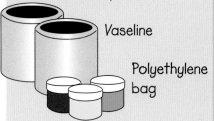

1 gallon cans or bigger

Enamel paints

Vaseline

Polyethylene bag

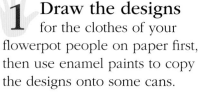

1 **Draw the designs** for the clothes of your flowerpot people on paper first, then use enamel paints to copy the designs onto some cans.

2 **Ask an adult** to make holes in the bottom of each can. Spread some gravel on the bottom for drainage. Now fill the cans with soil and water them thoroughly.

3 **Make two holes** ½in (1.5cm) deep near the center of each pot. Sow a seed in each hole and gently cover with soil. Cover the cans with a polyethylene bag with a few small holes in it.

4 **Cover the sides** of the cans with a ring of vaseline to deter slugs and position them in a sunny spot. Remove the bags when the seedlings' leaves appear and remove the weaker plant.

5 **Water little but often,** since without water sunflowers will quickly die. If your flowers have more than one head developing, cut the extra ones later for an indoor flower display.

6 **Once the sunflowers** have opened, use a pencil or pointed stick to pick out some of the tiny flowers on the head to make a face. Eyes, noses, and mouths can be different shapes.

Pets' corner

Why not grow some tasty treats for your pets? Cats, dogs, guinea pigs, and rabbits love to nibble plants, but it's important to provide them with ones they can eat safely. The grasses grown here provide nutrition for your pets as well.

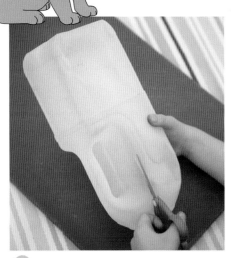

1 **For the labels,** cut a panel from a plastic milk carton and then draw an outline in the shape of your pet with a black marker.

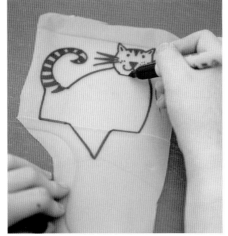

2 **Add features,** such as whiskers, eyes, nose, and a mouth, using the black marker. Then cut out the pet shape so it's ready as a label for the container.

3 **For each container,** ask an adult to drill some holes in the bottom. Fill with a little gravel and then add potting soil. Moisten the potting soil and let the water soak through.

4 **If the seeds are large,** such as cat grass for cats, push them slightly below the surface and then cover them with soil using your fingertips.

5 **If the seeds are small,** such Lucerne grass for dogs, sprinkle them over the surface of the moist potting soil and add a thin layer of soil on top.

6 **Keep the containers** well watered as the plants grow. Trim the plants using scissors to keep them at a good height for your pet.

Cat grass for your cat

Lucerne grass for your dog

For other pets ...

Sow barley, oats, and wheat for your rabbit.

Rabbit

Sow Timothy meadow grass and plantains for your guinea pigs.

Guinea pig

Plants for a fragrant garden

A garden is not just pretty—if you choose the right plants, it can also surround you with sweet smells all year round. The perfume comes from oils stored in the flower's petals that are released as it opens.

Roses

Flowers produce **strong scents** to attract insects and birds to pollinate them. When flowers smell nice, animals know there is pollen and nectar inside. As they land on each bloom, pollen clings to their feet and bodies and they carry it to the next flower. But not all flowers smell sweet—some give off a rotten scent to attract flies.

There are some plants that only open and release their scent at night. They do this to attract night-flying pollinators, such as moths and bats.

The classic **rose** fragrance is one of the best-loved scents. There are lots of different types of rose flower. They come in a range of colors, and some have petals that are particularly thick and velvety.

Freesia

Spring flower with a powerful scent.

Jasmine

Wonderful delicately scented white blooms.

Honeysuckle

Brightly colored, with honey-scented flowers.

Orchid

Orchids range in smell from fruity to spicy.

Fragrant flower gallery

Honeysuckle

Nicotiana

Lavender

Nicotiana blooms—also known as **flowering tobacco**—open and release their powerful fragrance when the Sun goes down. Nicotiana likes moist, fertile soil and is happiest growing in partial shade. Its flowers come in reds, pinks, whites, or greens.

Honeysuckle is a strong climber that is easy to grow. The vine produces bright flowers during the summer. Plant it in the ground, then train it up a trellis.

Lavender is a classic scented flower. It is native to North Africa and the area around the Mediterranean Sea, but is now loved all over the world..

Lavender buddy

You will need:

- old sock
- uncooked rice
- dried lavender flowers
- needle and thread
- stick-on eyes
- scraps of fabric
- pipe cleaners

Dry bunches of lavender by hanging them in a warm, dark place. After a month, they'll make good stuffing for this odd little character. He's made from an old sock—but the lavender makes him smell sweet!

1 **Fill a sock** with a mixture of rice and dried lavender flowers. The rice adds weight and helps the lavender go a bit further.

2 **Twist the end** of the sock to keep the lavender and rice in place. Secure it with a few stitches.

4 **Draw arms** and legs on fabric and cut them out. For thicker limbs, fold the fabric in half and cut through both layers. Then stitch around the edges.

5 **Attach the arms** and legs securely to the body with a few firm stitches.

6 **Make curly hair** for your lavender buddy by wrapping pipe cleaners around a pencil.

I'm made from a sock, too! The cardboard in my tail keeps it stiff, and my fins are candy wrappers.

3 **Now stitch** on a mouth using brightly colored thread. Peel the backs off the eyes and stick them in place.

7 **Sew the middles** of the pipe cleaners to the top of his head and bend them to make a wild hairstyle.

Enchanted path

Dance along your very own winding path through your backyard. Make these eye-catching stepping-stones by molding concrete into pretty leafy shapes. You'll need big leaves for this project, like the ones on rhubarb, zucchini, and sunflower plants.

You will need:
- disposable plastic gloves
- apron
- large plant leaves
- powdered cement mix
- large margarine container
- putty knife
- cardboard
- sand

1 **Mix up the cement** into a thick paste in a large margarine container according to the instructions on the packaging. Remember to wear an apron and disposable plastic gloves.

2 **For each stone,** lay one leaf flat on a large piece of cardboard. The leaf's veiny reverse side should be facing up.

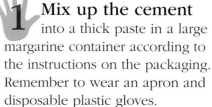

3 **With a putty knife,** spread the cement all over the leaf. This layer should be about ½in (1cm) thick at the edges, and at least 1½in (4cm) thick at the center.

4 **Smooth around** the edges and over the surface with your putty knife, then leave your concrete leaf for about two hours, until it's just dry enough to hold its shape.

5 **Gently turn it over and** peel away the leaf. This will be easier if the concrete is still a bit wet. Now leave the "stone" to dry completely for a day or two.

6 **Once your stones** are completely dry, decide on their position by arranging them on the grass to make sure their spacing suits your stride.

7 **Use a trowel** to mark around each shape. Remove the first stone and dig out the grass and soil to the depth of the stone plus an extra 1in (2.5cm).

To level the stones, add or remove sand underneath.

8 **Place a 1in (2.5cm) layer** of sand into each hole and make sure it's smooth before placing the stone on top. Repeat for all your stones, checking that they are not wobbly, and filling gaps around the edge with soil.

Top tip

Leave the stones to settle for a few days before walking on them.

Window box wildlife

Opening the curtains in the morning will be a whole new experience with bees, ladybugs, and butterflies flocking to your window box. Make your visitors feel at home with colorful flowers, lots of hiding places, and a nice drink of water.

Secure your crate to a sunny window ledge.

1 **If you are using** a wooden crate, put in a plastic liner with some holes to prevent the wood from rotting. Place rocks over the holes in the base and fill the container ¾ full of potting soil.

2 **First arrange** the plants, then make deep holes and place them in. Finally, fill in around the plant with soil, making sure the base of the stem where it meets the root is level with the soil's surface.

3 **Water the plants** well to help them settle in. Make sure space has been left at the top of the container so that the soil won't spill over when watering the plants for during heavy rain.

Use a flat stone to weigh the bottle down at the front end.

4 **Make a mini ladybug house** by folding some corrugated cardboard inside a bottle. Tilt the bottle downward among the plants to prevent water from getting inside.

5 **Place a small dish** or foil tray, sinking it into the soil. Fill it with water and place some small flat stones around the edge to look like a tiny pond.

6 **Tie together** some hollow sticks and dried seedpods for creatures to crawl into, and add a rock or two for them to crawl under. Once completed, place the window box on a flat surface.

We used lavender, chives, snapdragons, hebe, and ivy. These will encourage busy bees and fluttering butterflies—great pollinators. Lacewings and ladybugs will eat up pesky aphids. Many other beetles, and maybe a spider or two, may also pay you a visit.

Snapdragon

Dwarf hebe

Chives

Ivy

Lavender

Plants for a container pond

Aquatic plants are specially adapted to a watery environment and are vital ingredients for a pond. They provide oxygen, shade, shelter, and food for fish and other water creatures.

These plants provide useful resting places for dragonflies and their flowers are attractive to bees.

Marginal:
Greater spearwort
(Ranunculus lingua)

Emerging:
Sweet flag
(Acorus calamus)

Emerging:
Umbrella plant
(Cyperus alternifolius)

Emerging:
Duck potato
(Sagittaria latifolia)

Emerging plants
have roots in shallow water

Giant water lilies

Giant water lilies are truly enormous! Their leaves can grow up to 10ft (3m) across. They have white flowers that open at night and give out a scent to attract beetles. At daybreak, the flower closes, trapping the beetles, which become covered in pollen. The beetles are released later that evening and move on to pollinate a new flower. The flower then turns pink.

Turn to pages 62-63 to find out how to make your own container pond at home.

These plants provide shade for the pond.

Floating plants
have leaves that float on the surface

Oxygenating:
Hornwort
(*Ceratophyllum demersum*)

Marginal:
Bog primula
(*Primula florindae*)

Marginal:
Marsh marigold
(*Caltha palustris*)

Floating:
Frogbit
(*Hydrocharis morsus-ranae*)

Floating:
Water soldier
(*Stratiotes aloides*)

Marginal plants
like to live in wet, boggy soil

Oxygenating plants
live underwater

Container pond

This mini pond will fit on a patio or balcony. Put it in a shady place where it won't dry out, and set it up in its final position so you don't have to drag it when it's full of water.

Don't put too many plants in your pond—leave room for the fish!

1 **Arrange clean bricks** in the bottom of the container to make platforms for the plants. Put clean gravel in the bottom, then fill two-thirds full with rainwater.

2 **Put the oxygenating** plants, such as this hornwort, in first. Check the plant labels, since some types need to be anchored in the gravel, while others float freely in the water.

3 **Marginal plants**, such as sweet flag, go in next. Leave these in their pots, but put a layer of gravel on the soil to help keep it in place. Stand the pots on the bricks at the edge of the pond.

4 **You can group** marginal plants like marsh marigold and bog primula together. Line a plastic basket with sacking, fill with soil, then plant your plants. Finish with a layer of gravel.

5 **Fill the container** to the top with water. Then carefully place one or two floating plants on the surface. Make sure that some of the water surface is left clear of plants.

6 **Now add your fish!** Small goldfish or mosquito fish are perfect for mini ponds. They feed on mosquito larvae and algae. Move fish to a larger container as they grow.

Put a stick in your pond as an escape route for small creatures that fall in!

Carefully add your fish to the pond so you don't injure them. Lower the bag completely into the water and let the fish swim out.

Top tip
Fill or top off your pond with rainwater, since tap water often has chlorine in it, which can kill fish. If you have to use tap water, let it stand for a few days so the chlorine evaporates—then add your fish.

Corn paper

The leaves that are tightly wrapped around corncobs are called the husk. You can flatten these and paste them together to make paper. It takes about two weeks to dry, then you can use it to make beautiful gifts.

You will need:
- corn husks
- a large enamel or stainless-steel pan. Don't use an aluminum pan—the washing soda will ruin it
- washing soda (also called sodium carbonate)
- paper towels, old dish towels, and newspapers
- all-purpose flour

Wear rubber gloves during steps 2 and 3.

1 **Cut the top** and bottom off the corncob and carefully peel off the husk. Try to keep each leaf in one piece. Make sure you have an adult helping you.

2 **Fill a large pan** with water and stir in 1 tbsp washing soda for every 4 cups (1 liter) of water. Add the husks, bring to a boil, and simmer for about 30 minutes.

3 **Rinse the leaves** in plenty of cold water and let them drain on paper towels or on an old dish towel. Pat them as dry as possible with paper towels.

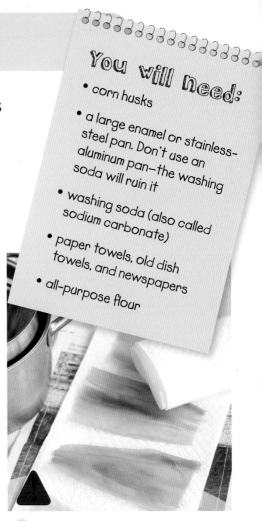

To make flour paste, mix together 1 tsp flour and 2 tsp water.

The finished paper

4 **Arrange the leaves** in a row so the edges overlap slightly. Stick the edges together with flour paste.

5 **Spread the leaves** with paste, then put another layer on top, at 90 degrees to the first. This is one sheet of paper.

6 **Sandwich** your paper between dish towels, then newspaper. Weight down with something heavy. Replace the newspaper when wet.

Gifts

Paint someone special a mini masterpiece on the paper you've made. You will need a frame and some acrylic paints and brushes.

Make a gift tag

Design a notebook

Cover a notebook with brown craft paper and glue a piece of corn paper on top. Paint a picture to decorate it.

Make a hole with a pen and thread some ribbon through each cover to finish the book.

Wild-West cacti

Yee-hah! Turn a container into a desert landscape by filling it with prickly cacti and other succulents. Because they store water in their fleshy leaves, stems, or roots, succulents can survive in harsh conditions such as deserts, scrublands, and mountains.

Horticultural sand   Perlite   Peat-based compost

Most cacti and succulents need soil that lets water drain away quickly to stop the plants from rotting. So use either a cactus potting mix, or create your own using equal amounts of peat-based compost and coarse sand. Add some perlite or vermiculite, since these also allow for quick draining.

Cover your cacti with clear plastic bottles or containers to keep them warm.

1 **Sprinkle a thin layer** of gravel into a seed tray. Most cacti have shallow roots because they store water in their stems. Add 1–2in (2–5cm) of cactus potting mix, and make holes for the plants.

2 **Beginning with the** largest cactus, ease each plant gently out of its old container. To do this, wear gloves and use tongs or wrap the cactus in newspaper, paper towels, or light cardboard.

3 **Place the first cactus** into its hole and use the back of a spoon to press the soil down around its base. Transplant the rest of the plants in the same way.

4 **Mist the soil or** sprinkle it lightly with lukewarm water. Repeat after the potting mix has looked very dry for a few days.

5 **Add details to make** your landscape look like the Wild West. Create a track using sand or gravel, for example, and add model figurines.

Place your landscape in a warm, partly shaded site.

This is a hairy trumpet cactus.

Plants for topiary

Topiary is the centuries-old art of clipping trees and shrubs into decorative shapes. It's also a way of training climbing plants around a frame. The result is anything from a neat pom-pom to an elephant.

Making shapes

Use a small-leaved evergreen plant. Since the leaves remain all year, so does your shape! You'll also need a wire frame to grow plants around or to use as a guide to cutting. Buy or make your frame.

A wire frame can be simple, like a heart, or more complicated, like this seahorse. Wrap the plant around the frame as it grows. Snip off any shoots growing in the wrong direction.

For clipped topiary, put your frame over the plant. Snip the plant to the shape of the frame.

Trim little and often as your plant takes shape.

Chicken

Cone

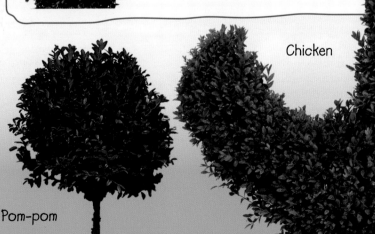

Pom-pom

Privet

Traditionally used
for garden hedges.

Yew

A dense, slow-
growing evergreen.

Box

Good for small topiary.

Shrubby honeysuckle

A fast-growing
hedging plant.

Juniper

A hardy plant
with dense leaves.

Choose a healthy plant with an even shape

Plant watch

When you snip
your plant, keep the cuts
neat—ragged edges look
untidy. Ideally trim in early
summer. Never trim when
there is a frost, since this
can damage the plant.

Topiarists trim their creations
using scissors, pruners, or hand
shears. Electric hedge trimmers can
also be used for
large creations.

Topiary shears

Elephant
and rider

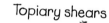

Spiral
topiary

Important stuff

Ivy grows best out of direct sunlight. Keep in a sheltered place.

Water ivy when the soil begins to feel dry—but don't let it dry out.

The ivy should cover the frame in 2 to 3 months.

Ivy man

If you don't want to wait for years for a topiary figure to take shape, try your hand at this ivy man. He's made from a wire frame and will spring to life in just a few months.

You will need:

- garden wire
- scissors or wire cutters
- window box or similar container
- all-purpose potting soil
- small stick
- metal food tray
- two small-leaved ivy plants

1 For the head, ask an adult to help you twist a length of wire into an oval, leaving enough wire to make the neck. Make sure your ivy man is the right size to fit the container.

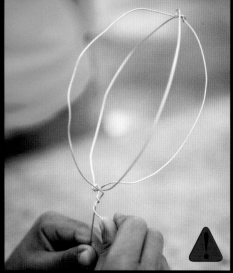

2 Take another length of wire and make a second oval, twisting it around the first to make a 3-D head. Secure it at the neck.

4 Fill a container with all-purpose potting soil. Position your ivy man. To help him stand up, try making a shovel from a stick and metal food tray. Plant the ivy.

5 Plant ivy at the base of each leg and wrap the tendrils around the frame.

Plant watch

Ivy is a climbing plant that loves to scramble up walls, trees, and fences. It can reach as high as 100ft (30m) above the ground. Ivy hauls itself up using aerial roots that grow along its stem. These help the plant to grip the surface.

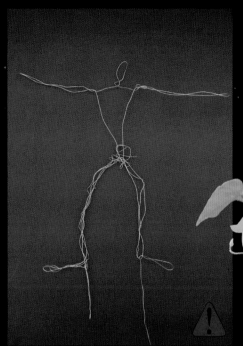

3 **Make the body** by twisting more wire into a body shape. Include spikes to anchor the frame in the ground. Attach the body to the head and wrap more wire around the whole thing.

6 **As the ivy grows,** thread it through the frame. Clip out any shoots that are growing in the wrong direction. After a few months, ivy will cover the whole frame.

71

Insect-eating plant

Here's a mini world in a jar, and the plant at the center is an insect-eating sundew. Sit it on a sunny windowsill and sticky droplets form on its leaves. Passing insects stick to these and are digested to death. Team up the sundew with modeling clay aliens to make a bottle garden that's out of this world!

Sundews like to live in a sunny spot.

Keep well watered. Sundews only drink soft water or rain water.

Some sundews can live for up to 50 years.

You will need:

- aquarium gravel or recycled beads and stones
- large plastic storage jar
- glitter
- carnivorous plant potting mix
- sundew carnivorous plant
- modeling clay

1 **Start by dropping** colored gravel into the bottom of your storage jar. Make layers using different colors and sprinkle on glitter for sparkle.

2 **Now drop in handfuls** of potting mix. Press it down gently. Make sure you leave enough room for the sundew!

4 **Make your alien.** No one knows what an alien looks like, so they can be any shape you like! Squash some modeling clay into a body and add eyes, arms, and legs.

5 **Here's one we made** earlier. Think about where your alien will go. Inside the jar? Sticking to the outside? This will help you decide how big to make it.

Look out alien dragonfly—there's a sticky trap below!

3 **Remove the sundew** from its pot, plant it in the middle of the potting mix, and firm the potting mix gently around it.

Small fly

6 **Leave your alien** world to settle. The sundew will start to form new droplets on its leaves that small flies will stick to.

Top tip

Carnivorous plants usually like a peat and sand mix of potting soil. You can buy it ready mixed, or make your own using two parts moss peat to one part sand.

Bug quiz

Are insects the only bugs?

The word "bugs" can include not just insects, but also other creepy crawlies that have no backbones, such as scorpions, millipedes, and woodlice.

5 FACTS ABOUT BUTTERFLIES

- There are 20,000 different species all over the world.

- We eat flower nectar (a sweet liquid) and pollen (a fine powder).

- Most of us live in tropical rainforests.

- We are very light.

- We are eaten by birds.

Why don't spiders get stuck in their own webs?

Only some of the silky strands on spider webs are sticky for catching insects. Spiders don't step on these. We may also use some of our tiny claws on our feet to lift the sticky strands out of the way.

5 FACTS ABOUT BUGS

- There are well over a million species around the world.

- Insects are the largest group of bug.

- Many bugs eat plants, some eat other insects, and others eat blood, dung, or decaying matter.

- Some of us can bite and sting, while others can pinch with our mouthparts.

- We shed our skin (molt) as we grow, sometimes completely transforming for our last adult stage.

Why are butterflies so colorful?

Colorful wings are very important to us. Our colors help us to hide ourselves or startle enemies. They help us to keep us warm and to attract mates.

5 FACTS ABOUT SPIDERS

- There are 40,000 species of spider.

- Most of us live on our own.

- Most species live for 1-2 years, but tarantulas can live much longer.

- Different species eat different things.

- Female spiders lay more than 1,000 eggs at a time and wrap them in a silk egg sac.

5 FACTS ABOUT ANTS

- There are about 35,000 species of ant.

- We are found all over the world, except Antarctica.

- Our nests can be found in trees, just below the soil, or deep underground.

- Only the queen ant lays eggs.

- One of our main enemies is other ants.

Do all bees make honey?

Very few bees make honey, and only honeybees store enough for you to take some, too. I am a bumblebee and I only make about ½ teaspoon of honey in my lifetime.

5 FACTS ABOUT BEES

- There are about 2,000 species of bee around the world.

- We feed on pollen and nectar.

- We help plants to make fruit by pollinating them.

- Our young are called larvae.

- We have many enemies, such as frogs, toads, and insect-eating birds, plus bugs, including wasps and spiders.

Why do ants have armies?

We are social insects, which means we live in a group, or colony, to help us survive. We each have a job to do. Most of us are workers but some are soldiers, guarding the nest. Soldier ants defend the colony by biting, stinging, or spraying acid on attackers.

5 FACTS ABOUT DRAGONFLIES

- There are more than 5,000 different species.

- We can be found on every continent except Antarctica.

- We eat other insects, such as mosquitoes, midges, and spiders.

- We have been around for 300 million years.

- We do not harm people.

Are all ladybugs spotted?

Most ladybugs have spots, but not all of us do. The ladybugs with the most spots have 24. But there are a few of us who have white stripes instead of black spots, and some of us have no markings at all.

5 FACTS ABOUT Ladybugs

- There are over 5,000 species all over the world.

- We are beetles.

- We live in trees, shrubs, fields, beaches, and even in your home.

- We eat garden pests, such as aphids, mealybugs, and mites.

- Most of us don't bite.

Why are all dragonflies in a hurry?

We don't have very long to live as adults, so we zoom around finding food and a mate. The largest dragonflies can fly up to 25–38 mph (40–60 km/h), making us the fastest flying insects.

Cool plants to grow

Get ready to impress your friends with some unusual plants, from ones that look, smell, or feel strange to those with surprising behavior. Some can be grown from seed or bought in stores, while others can be started in pretty unusual ways.

1

Tickle-me plant *Mimosa pudica*

 Germinates in 2-3 weeks | 12in (30cm)

When touched, the fernlike leaves of this very sensitive plant curl up, setting off a chain reaction where nearby leaf stalks of the plant fold in, too. The leaves also fold over in the dark. If touched too many times, the plant's reaction may slow down.

2

Coleus *Coleus blumei*

Germinates in 2 weeks | Dwarf and tall varieties

Grown indoors or outdoors, this eye-catching plant has dramatic, colorful leaves. Encourage the plant to become bushy and last longer by pinching out the small flowers and growing shoots at the end of summer.

3

Avocado pit *Persea americana*

Germinates in 6 weeks | Very tall tree

Impress yourself as well as your friends by growing your own avocado plant from its pit. Push three toothpicks into the center of the pit (pointed end upward), and place over a jar full of water so that the pit dips in. A seedling will form.

6

Ornamental gourds *Curcurbita pepo*

Germinates in 2 weeks | Height varies

There's an impressive array of strangely shaped, colored, and patterned gourds to choose from. In the fall, they can be dried to make interesting hanging decorations or the larger gourds can be hollowed out to become quirky plant containers.

7

Pineapple top *Ananas comosus*

 Rooting: in 6-8 weeks | 12in (30cm)

Slice the leafy top off a fresh pineapple, strip away a few leaves at the base, let dry, and then place into a pot with potting soil and keep moist. Hey presto—within six weeks the top will start to root! Although it will be a year or two before it fruits.

8

Chocolate cosmos *Cosmos atrosanguineus*

Germinates in 5-10 days | 3ft (90cm)

The dark brown-red flowers of this perennial plant produce a powerful smell of vanilla and sweet chocolate. Originally from Mexico, the plant is no longer found in the wild. The blooms last through the summer and into the fall.

4

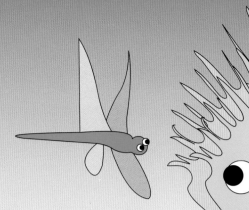

Lablab beans *Lablab purpureus*

Germinates in 2-3 weeks | 6ft (2m)

Lablab beans are climbing plants that produce pods that can be eaten when cooked. They have stunning purple and pink fragrant flowers followed by fascinating dark purple seedpods, all surrounded by green and purple-brown leaves.

5

Corn *Zea mays*

Germinates in 1-2 weeks | 5ft (1.5m)

Sow corn kernels bought from a pet store in a container. Place each about 4in (10cm) apart and, if kept moist, fertilized, and warm, in about 3 months corncobs will be ready to harvest. It's a-maize-ing!

9

Venus flytrap *Dionaea muscipula*

Germinates in 4-6 weeks | 6in (15cm)

Venus flytraps survive by feeding on flies and other insects. Their reactions are fascinating to watch. You can feed your plant, if you like. Using tweezers, place an insect inside its head-trap every 10 days. Do not touch the trigger hairs.

10

Lemon verbena *Alpysia triphylla*

Germinates in 2-3 weeks | A bushy shrub

If you rub your fingers on the leaves of the lemon verbena plant, they will pick up a powerful smell of lemon. On page 33, we've used these leaves to flavor herbal teas. They can also be added to potpourris. New plants can be grown from cuttings.

Glossary

Annual
A plant that completes its whole life cycle in a year.

Aquatic plant
A plant whose roots are permanently underwater. The rest of the plant may also be fully submerged or float on the surface.

Cactus
A spiny plant that can store water inside its stem.

Carnivorous plant
A plant that captures and eats insects to obtain nutrients that it cannot get from the soil.

Compost
Potting compost, or potting soil, is a special soil mix for growing plants in pots. Garden compost is a soil improver made from decayed plants.

Fertilizer
A mixture that encourages plants to grow.

Flower
This is the structure that contains the male and female parts of the plant.

Fruit
The part of a plant that forms when a flower is pollinated. The fleshy part protects the seeds inside.

Germination
When seeds sprout and start to grow.

Grasses
A family of flowering plants that has narrow leaves growing from the base. Cereal crops, such as wheat and barley, are grasses.

Green gardening
A way of gardening that is environmentally friendly, encouraging wildlife and using homemade compost rather than artificial chemicals.

Leaf
The part of a plant that makes the plant's food through a process called photosynthesis. A leaf takes in carbon dioxide from the air and uses sunlight to join this with water to make sugar-based food.

Moist
Slightly wet.

Mulch
A thick layer covering the surface of the soil that keeps in the moisture, prevents weeds from growing, and helps protect the roots from cold. Some add nutrients to the soil.

Pests
Any bug or animal in the garden that harms plants.

Pesticide
A chemical that is used to kill insects, slugs, snails, and other small creatures that damage plants.

Pollination
The process of transferring pollen from the male part of a flower to the female part so that seeds can be produced.

Roots
The underground parts of a plant that take up minerals and water from the soil and support the plant. Enlarged roots, such as carrots, store food and water.

Seed
A part of a flowering plant that contains a baby plant and a store of food to get it started.

Sprout
A seed that has just begun to germinate.

Topiary
Cutting trees and shrubs so that they grow into interesting shapes.

Transplant
To move a young plant that has outgrown its pot into a larger container.

Vegetable
The edible leaf, stem, or root of a plant. Some plants that are commonly called vegetables, such as peppers and tomatoes, are actually fruits.

Index

Acknowledgments

Dorling Kindersley would like to thank:

**Photographer
Will Heap
www.willheap.com**

• Vauxhall City Farm for use of their allotments for additional photography. Dianne Sullock, Sharon Clouston, and Bernadette Kennedy from Vauxhall City Farm

• Capel Manor College for the use of their garden and for taking care of our plants. The Capel Manor Team: Tony Monaghan, Sarah Neophytou, and Joanna Bates

• Brockwell Community Greenhouses for the use of their area, and especially to Fabrice Boltho and Dianne Sullock, the site supervisers, for helping us to arrange location usage

• Steiner Hoathly Hill Community in West Sussex for use of their grounds

• Antonia Salt at Green Ink

• Brockwell Community Greenhouses

• Roots and Shoots

• Alleyn Park Garden Centre Ltd.

• Garsons Farm Shop

• The Garlic Farm

• Defland Nurseries Ltd.

• Keift & Sons Ltd. for supplies

• Annie Nichols for food styling

• Kate Heap for props and styling

• Secret Seed Society for providing all the plant characters in this book

• RAGT Seeds for supplying wheat products

• Meredith Mistry for making sweet-smelling lavender buddies

• David Crawford for making corn paper

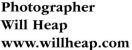

• Jim Arbury, RHS Wisley, for supplying loofah plants

• The staff at Shoots Garden Centre, Stanmore, Middlesex, for plants and advice

• David Arnold, Sutton Seeds, for supplying tomato, corn, and bell pepper plants

• Jon Wheatley and Mary Payne MBE, horticultural consultant, Stonebarn Landscapes Limited, for supplying vegetable plants

• Hannah and Molly for illustrating the corn paper and notebooks on page 65

• Our models: Cherry, Camron, Molly, Sophia, Zeynep, Christian, Solly, Omid Alavi, Rhianna Bryan, Cara Crosby-Irons, Scarlet and Stanley Heap, Fiona Lock, Kieran and Jane Mistry, Hannah and Max Moore, Matthew Morley, Jamie Chang-Leng, Spencer Britton, Kitty Nallet, Saphira Noor, Julia Scott, Alfred and Molly Warren

Picture credits

Thank you, everyone!

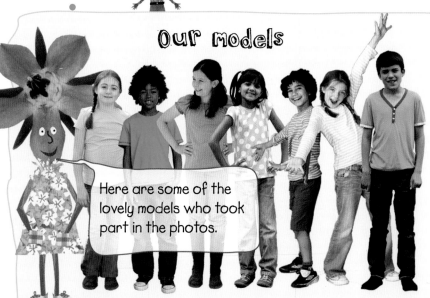

Our models

Here are some of the lovely models who took part in the photos.

Cherry Camron   Sophia Zeynep Christian Hannah Solly